Made by yourself

Peter Fehrentz

Made by *yourself*

100% Handmade Designer DIY Projects for the
Home, from Furniture to Accessories

jacqui
small

You can get ideas for your own creations practically everywhere: in the DIY store, at the scrap yard, at the flea market and in places you would never expect to find inspiration. It is fun to experiment with different materials and to put them in a new and unexpected context.

Sometimes an idea is very simple but it may turn out to be quite complicated to realize. You may have to tinker with it for quite a while until it looks the way you envisaged it. But at the end of the day, you can be proud to have created something all by yourself: an object to give to a friend or to enhance your own space with. *Made by Yourself* is a book for everyone who loves to take a new and creative look at things.

In the following eight chapters, I will present a range of ideas for furniture and design objects, discussing the necessary tools and materials and explaining step by step how to make each project. Each chapter is dedicated to a different material. It is not really necessary to follow the instructions to the letter. Rather, this book is meant to inspire you. A good cook does not religiously follow a recipe, but will add an individual touch to every dish, thereby making it truly exceptional and uniquely their own. The same principle applies to every creative action. Dare to be different!

Peter Fehrentz

647060

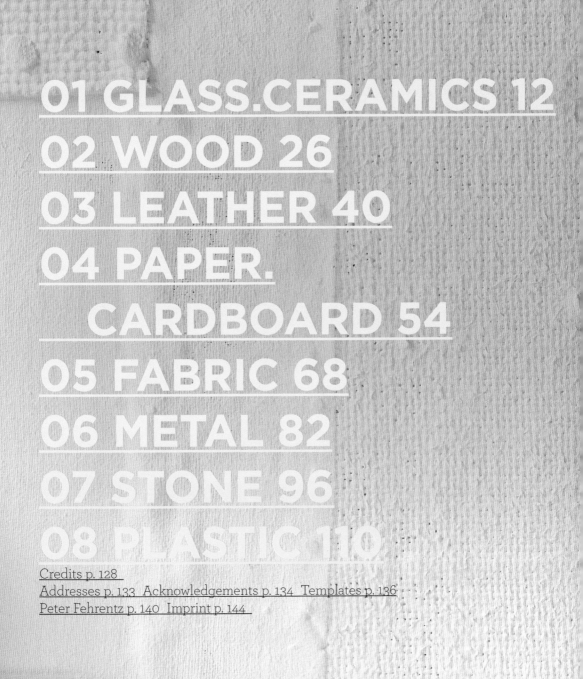

LEVEL 05   TIME 03 H   COST 02

All projects are rated according to how difficult it is to realize them, how much time it takes to make them and how much it would cost. The time will be measured in hours (H), the skill level and cost is rated on a scale from 01 (easy) to 06 (difficult). However, these are just rough guides. There may be significant regional variations, especially with regard to cost. Have fun with the projects!

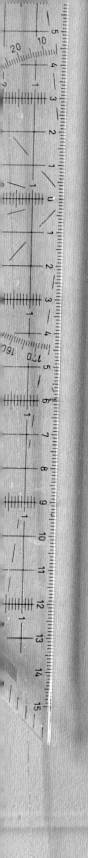

01

Glass
Ceramics

Cake Stand

You can find pretty individual plates in charity shops or car boot sales. This stunning creation will take the cake at tea time!

LEVEL 05   TIME 03 H   COST 02

Step 01 / Turn each plate over and mark the centre. Slowly and carefully drill a hole through each one, using a porcelain drill bit. Use a drill stand to stabilize the work and occasionally spray with water to cool.

Step 02 / Determine the space between the tiers of your cake stand and cut the aluminium tube into four corresponding lengths.

Step 03 / Colour the tube lengths, washers, screw nuts and ring nuts with spray paint.

Step 04 / Feed the threaded rod through the largest plate and secure with a screw nut underneath. Then slip a washer, a length of tube, a washer, the next largest plate and so forth onto the rod. Trim the rod about 5 mm above the last piece of tube with a hacksaw. Screw the ring nut on tightly to stabilize the assemblage.

Tip / When using neon spray paint, you need to apply a base coat to bring out the brightness of the colours.

MATERIALS
4 different-sized plates,
threaded rod diameter 10 mm,
aluminium tubing diameter 12 mm,
washers, flat screw nut diameter 10 mm,
ring nut diameter 10 mm (10 mm thread),
spray paint, water for cooling

TOOLS
Ceramic drill bit diameter 12 mm,
electric drill, drill stand,
hacksaw

Drop-shaped
Mirrors

Who says mirrors have to be round or square?
Your glazier will be happy to cut your mirrors to
any shape you wish.

LEVEL 04   TIME 02 H   COST 04

Step 01 / When you bring both ends of the balsa wood strip together, it will naturally form a perfect drop. Trace the shape onto a sheet of paper, then fold the paper in half lengthwise and cut out both sides together. The outline will now be perfectly symmetrical. Trace the shape three times onto a piece of chipboard and cut out with a jigsaw.

Step 02 / Ask the glazier to cut three mirrors with bevelled edges to size.

Step 03 / With the help of a craft knife and a straight edge, cut the balsa wood strips into three different widths.

Step 04 / Shape the strips into drops again and secure with masking tape at the tips. Glue the frames to the chipboard along the bottom edges. Glue the mirror to the chipboard. Leave to dry thoroughly.

Tip / Alternatively, make the mirrors in three different sizes. Take care that the circumference of the largest drop does not exceed the length of the balsa strip.

MATERIALS
Mirror, chipboard 80 x 45 cm, 20 mm thickness, 3 balsa wood strips 10 x 100 cm, strong adhesive, paper, masking tape

TOOLS
Jigsaw, craft knife, straight edge

See-through Picture Frames

A new and interesting way to mount dried leaves and delicate flowers.

LEVEL 01   TIME 03 H   COST 02

Step 01 / Carefully press the plants individually between layers of newspaper and cardboard, weighted down evenly with books, bricks or the like. Leave to dry for at least one week.

Step 02 / Arrange the dried plants on a sheet of glass. Secure with a few drops of glue at the back if necessary. Cover with another sheet of glass.

Step 03 / With the help of long-nose pliers, make u-shaped wire hooks, leaving 3 cm ends sticking out at right angles. These will anchor the hooks to the fabric-tape frame.

Step 04 / Cut the fabric tape to the measurements of the frame sides. Mitre-cut the corners. About 4 cm in from the top edges of the frame, cut two small slits into the corresponding tape to accommodate the hooks. Slide the hooks into the slits and tape the two glass panes together all the way round.

Tip / Use delicate plants, which can be pressed very flat.

MATERIALS
Glass sheets (2 for each picture), fabric tape, pressed plants, newspaper, cardboard, wire, all-purpose glue

TOOLS
Long-nose pliers, craft knife, weights

Display Cases

Glass cases made to measure: a perfect way to display your curios and prized possessions.

LEVEL 06   TIME 05 H   COST 06

Step 01 / Choose the measurements for your display case and mitre-cut the angular sections at both ends. Finely sand down all edges and surfaces with a metal file and fine-grade abrasive paper.

Step 02 / Assemble one side of the case and measure the outside dimensions. The corresponding glass pane must be 4 mm smaller. Repeat with the remaining sides.

Step 03 / Assemble two sides of the case, spread a fine line of silicone along the inside edges of the angular sections and carefully glue the glass into the frame. Leave to dry overnight.

Step 04 / Hold the two sides upright facing each other and connect with angular sections at the bottom. Secure the sides with masking tape, making sure they are at right angles to each other. Glue in one side pane and leave to dry. Turn the assemblage over and glue in the remaining glass pane. Attach the top pane in the same way.

Step 05 / Cut a piece of MDF according to the inside measurements of the case, and another piece that is 2 cm wider on all sides. Glue the smaller piece onto the larger piece and leave to dry. Apply a couple of coats of glossy acrylic paint.

Tip / When in doubt, have the mitres cut at your wood store – they have all the right equipment and the job will be done much faster!

MATERIAL

Picture glass 2 mm thickness, brass angular sections 15 x 15 x 1.5 mm, transparent silicone, MDF board 22 mm, acrylic paint, masking tape

TOOLS

Glass cutter, mitre or jigsaw, metal file, circular saw, silicone cartridge gun, paint brush, fine-grade metal abrasive paper

Wall Plates

These plates are very easy to create and they make ideal presents. Be sure to make enough of them to keep some for yourself!

LEVEL 02   TIME 03 H   COST 03

Step 01 / Thoroughly clean the plate with window-cleaning liquid.

Step 02 / Print your chosen design onto the ceramic transfer paper and allow the ink to dry for a few minutes.

Step 03 / Peel off the backing paper and place the design on the ceramic decal paper. Carefully smooth out creases and air bubbles. Cover with tracing paper and iron at 160 °C wihout steam for about 10 – 15 seconds to fuse the layers.
Do not move the iron during this time to keep the design pristine.

Step 04 / Leave to cool, then carefully cut out the design, leaving a margin of about 10 mm around it.

Step 05 / Steep the paper in lukewarm water for a few minutes until the design comes off easily. Slip the design onto the plate and position, then carefully press out excess water with a soft cloth. Leave to dry for at least 10 hours.

Step 06 / Preheat the oven to 150 – 170 °C, set the plate onto the middle rack and fire for 25 – 30 minutes. Carefully press down any parts of the design that may have come off the plate using a wooden spoon.

Step 07 / Attach plate hooks onto the upper back of the plate with power glue. Repeat as desired.

Tip / Flat plates are best for this kind of project.

MATERIALS
Transfer paper, ceramic decal paper, plates and plate hooks, power adhesive, tracing paper

TOOLS
Scissors, bowl with warm water, cloth, window-cleaning liquid, iron

Chandelier

All you need to make this spectacular chandelier is a simple light bulb and some window glass.

LEVEL 02   TIME 04 H   COST 02

Step 01 / With the help of a straight edge and a glass cutter, score the glass into 2–3 cm strips. Break the strips apart over the edge of a tabletop.

Step 02 / Score the strips into 3–8 cm pieces and break them apart as described in step 1. Smooth all the edges lightly with sanding paper.

Step 03 / Connect the textile cable to the light socket. Make three wire loops (about 8, 10 and 12 cm in diameter). Attach two lengths of wire (about 15 cm each) crosswise to the textile cable to secure the wire loops. Attach the three loops in concentric order on the cross-wires with fine wire.

Step 04 / Attach strips of packing tape to a large enough work surface (this allows the glass strips to be easily removed later on). Lay out the glass rectangles in 20–40 cm strips. Spread very fine lines of transparent silicone between the spaces and carefully push the pieces together. Leave to dry overnight.

Step 05 / Trim the excess silicone with a craft knife and carefully remove the glass strips from the tape. Attach the glass strips to the wire loops with Sellotape — the longer strips on the inside and the shortest on the outside.

Tip / Use coloured glass for a completely different look.

MATERIALS
Textile cable, ceramic light socket and light bulb, glass off-cuts 2 mm thickness, transparent silicone, wire diameter 1 mm, parcel tape, Sellotape

TOOLS
Glass cutter, cutting board, pliers, silicone cartridge gun, craft knife, straight edge, fine-grade abrasive paper

02
Wood

Suitcase
Side Table

You just need a suitcase, four table legs and some spray paint to make this wonderful occasional table. But don't lose the key!

LEVEL 01   TIME 02 H   COST 03

Step 01 / Paint the table legs to match the colour of the suitcase, but leave the bottom unpainted. For a smooth transition move the spray can away from the object as you paint.

Step 02 / Position the leg brackets diagonally onto the four courners at the bottom of the suitcase. Drill holes in the bottom of the suitcase and attach the brackets from the inside with wood screws and washers.

Step 03 / Seal the table legs with a coat of transparent varnish.

Step 04 / Screw the legs into the brackets.

Tip / Table legs are available in a wide variety of styles and materials to match every suitcase you can find.

MATERIAL
Suitcase, wooden table legs with brackets, wood screws, washers, high-gloss spray paint, transparent varnish

TOOLS
Electric drill, cordless screwdriver

Inlaid Table

You often find perfectly serviceable tables with ugly tops at charity shops or flea markets. They deserve a second chance!

LEVEL 02   TIME 05 H   COST 05

Step 01 / Sketch a geometric design to fit the tabletop. Transfer the shapes (here, equilateral triangles) onto the back of the wood veneer and cut out with a craft knife.

Step 02 / Sand the tabletop to obtain a smooth surface and paint the table frame with acrylic gloss paint. Mark the centre of the tabletop.

Step 03 / Starting from the centre, spread wood glue onto the tabletop with a brush and carefully lay out the veneer pieces. Work in sections and weight down the surface evenly to allow the veneer to dry flat.

Step 04 / When thoroughly dry, finely sand the surface and seal with linseed oil.

Tip / Fill small gaps with a mixture of sanding dust and wood glue. Sand down evenly when dry.

MATERIALS

Second-hand table, Decoflex veneer, wood glue, high-gloss acrylic paint, linseed oil

TOOLS

Craft knife, set square abrasive paper, paintbrush, pencil

Table from Wood Offcuts

A beautiful and rock-solid side table – this is recycling at its best!

LEVEL 01   TIME 02 H   COST 01

Step 01 / With a circular saw, cut the wood offcuts into 5–20 cm sections. Cut the squared timber into two 40 cm lengths. Cut two 40 x 40 cm pieces for the top and bottom of the table.

Step 02 / The squared timber lengths serve as the middle column. Attach them to the top and bottom with two long wood screws each.

Step 03 / From the centre outwards, arrange the wooden offcuts as desired and attach with fast-drying wood glue. Temporarily secure with masking tape if necessary.

Step 04 / Add further layers of wood pieces until the table is roughly cube-shaped .

Tip / Turn the table over in order to glue down the topmost pieces.

MATERIAL
Wood offcuts, squared timber ca. 80 x 15 x 8 cm, long wood screws, wood glue, masking tape

TOOLS
Circular table saw or jigsaw, cordless screwdriver

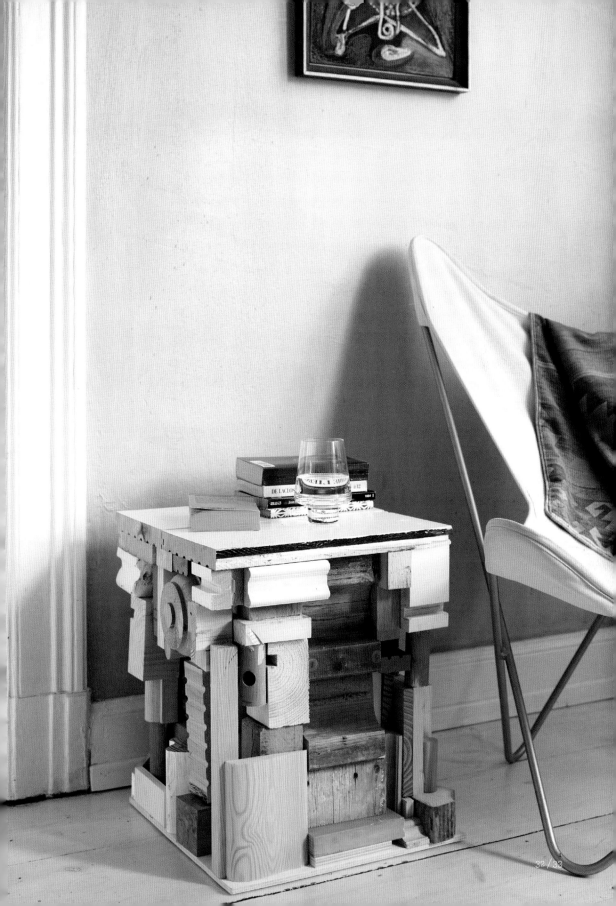

Banister Candlesticks

Beautifully turned old banister rails make fantastic candlesticks – the more, the merrier!

LEVEL 02   TIME 03–04 H   COST 03

Step 01 / Cut the rails into 15 – 35 cm lengths and sand down all edges and surfaces.

Step 02 / Drill a hole into the top of each rail with a Forstner drill bit – the holes need to be a few millimetres deeper than the candle cups.

Step 03 / Paint the candlesticks to taste. For crisp lines, use masking tape.

Step 04 / When the paint is dry, glue the candle cups into the holes with hot glue.

Tip / Make sure to press down the edges of the masking tape thoroughly to prevent bleeding. Apply several thin coats of paint rather than one thick coat.

MATERIALS
Turned banister rails, candle cups, acrylic paint, masking tape, hot glue

TOOLS
Wood saw, electric drill and Forstner drill bit diameter 22 mm, hot glue gun, paintbrush, abrasive paper

Plank Bench

Old scaffolding planks have a story to tell – the perfect material to make into a reading bench!

LEVEL 01   TIME 01 H   COST 01

Step 01 / With a hacksaw, cut four plank segments to the desired measurements.

Step 02 / Using wood screws, assemble the bench as shown in the large image. Drilling pilot holes beforehand prevents the boards from splitting.

Step 03 / Strengthen the left and right corners underneath with metal brackets.

Tip / Seal the wood surface with beeswax or matte varnish.

MATERIALS
Old scaffolding planks,
metal brackets, wood screws,
beeswax or matte varnish

TOOLS
Hacksaw, cordless screwdriver,
electric drill and wood drill bit
diameter 3 mm

Tray with Marquetry Design

Beautiful trays in different sizes make fine displays for dishes, cutlery and spices.

LEVEL 02   TIME 02 H   COST 03

Step 01 / Cut pre-fabricated marquetry strips to fit the side measurements of the tray.

Step 02 / Attach the strips to the tray with wood glue and secure with masking tape. Leave to dry for a few hours. Lightly sand with fine-grade abrasive paper.

Step 03 / Seal the trays with clear varnish.

Tip / For extra effect, you can paint the inside of the tray with matching colours.

MATERIALS
Wooden tray, marquetry strips, wood glue, clear varnish, masking tape

TOOLS
Craft knife, paintbrush, fine-grade abrasive paper

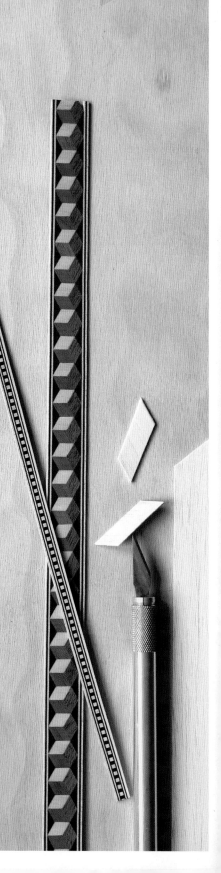

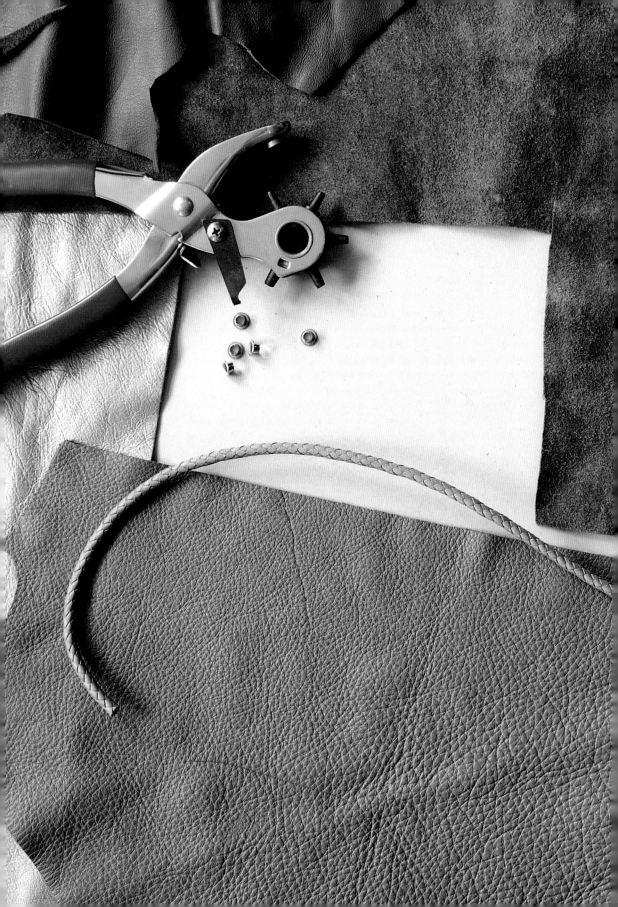

03
Leather

Herringbone Cushion

Leather off-cuts can be used to great effect!

LEVEL 02-03   TIME 03 H   COST 02

Step 01 / Trace a 40 x 40 cm square and two 20 x 40 cm rectangles for the back of the cushion onto the felt. Cut out with a seam allowance of approximately 1 cm.

Step 02 / Cut a sufficiently large piece of leather into 7 x 3.5 cm rectangles.

Step 03 / Glue the rectangles to the felt in a herringbone pattern as shown. Leave a small space between the rectangles. Do not spread the glue all the way to the edges of the leather to allow the corners to turn up slightly.

Step 04 / Sew a zipper between the two smaller felt rectangles.

Step 05 / Sew the two sides of the cushion Cover together with right sides facing, leaving the zip slightly open to allow turning the cover inside out.

Tip / If you are using the cushion on a daily basis, it is better to sew the leather to the felt backing.

MATERIALS
Leather, felt, seam ripper,
sewing thread, textile glue,
cushion 40 x 40 cm, tailor's chalk,
invisible zip (optional)

TOOLS
Craft knife or scissors,
set square, sewing machine and
special foot for invisible zip
(optional)

Polygonal Leather Boxes

You can never have enough small containers for your odds and ends – and these are extra stylish.

LEVEL 02   TIME 03 H   COST 03

Step 01 / Draw several polygonal shapes on paper. Be sure to leave enough space between them for the side parts. For the side parts, draw lines at right angles to the lines of the polygons to the desired length and connect them with a parallel line.

Step 02 / Trace the design onto the leather and cut out with a craft knife and the help of a set square.

Step 03 / With punch pliers, make holes (about 3 mm) along the bottom and sides of the leather pieces. The holes should be evenly spaced (about 1 cm apart).

Step 04 / Lace the pieces together with the string and tie off securely.

Tip / For a different effect, use string in a contrasting colour.

MATERIALS
Sturdy shoe leather, paper,
sturdy yarn or string

TOOLS
Craft knife, punch pliers,
set square, pencil

Leather Flowers

Give simple vases a bespoke look with a colourful
array of leather flowers.

LEVEL 01   TIME 02 H   COST 02

Step 01 / With a craft knife, cut 2–4 cm leather strips about
20–30 cm in length. Fold the strips lengthwise, wrong sides
facing, and glue together along the bottom.

Step 02 / Cut parallel lines along the top fold to about 2/3 of the
width of the strip.

Step 03 / Roll the strip into a flower, pushing up the inside slightly
for a three-dimensional effect. Secure the bottom with glue.

Step 04 / Glue a leather circle over the bottom part and attach the
flowers to the vase with double-sided tape.

Tip / Glue snap fasteners to the vase and the underside of the
flowers. This allows the flowers to be easily removed from the
vase for cleaning.

MATERIALS
Leather off-cuts in different
colours, leather glue, vases,
double-sided tape, snap
fasteners (optional)

TOOLS
Craft knife, cutting board

Leather Chair

You often find chairs and stools with damaged seats by the side of the road. With a little bit of skill, you can give them a spectacular makeover.

LEVEL 04   TIME 03 H   COST 05-06

Step 01 / Remove the damaged seat and back and trace the outlines on paper. Add a seam allowance of about 2 cm to the parts that attach to the chair.

Step 02 / Remove all traces of the old upholstery. Sand down all surfaces, removing the old paint or varnish.

Step 03 / Paint the chair in your chosen colour and leave to dry thoroughly.

Step 04 / Trace the paper pattern onto the leather and cut it out with a craft knife on a cutting board.

Step 05 / Nail the leather to the chair at the appropriate places. This is easier to do with the help of another person.

Tip / Use cowhide for a dramatic effect. Make sure that it is strong enough for the purpose.

MATERIALS
Old chair, thick saddle leather, short steel pins, paper, acrylic paint

TOOLS
Craft knife, hammer, cutting board, abrasive paper, paintbrush

Bench with Woven Seat

Update a simple, mass-produced bench with a
woven leather seat, turning it into a prized original.

LEVEL 03   TIME 04 H   COST 04–05

Step 01 / Assemble the bench according to the instructions, but
leave out the seat.

Step 02 / The round belts need to be at least 120 cm long to
cover the length of the bench. Attach the belts 2 cm apart along
the bottom of one side of the frame with steel nails, then stretch
them taut and nail to the other side. Do not overstretch. Trim
the excess with a craft knife.

Step 03 / Nail the belts along one long side in the same way
as in step 02, weave through and nail to the other long side.
Take care not to pull the belts too taut towards the middle of
the bench or the frame might warp. It helps to have two pairs of
hands for this project: one to pull the leather belts taut and the
other to nail them down.

Step 04 / Cut leather rectangles to cover the corners of the seat
and fix them in place with craft glue.

Tip / The bench will curve slightly inwards towards the
middle because of the strong tension of the leather straps, but
this only adds to the charm.

MATERIALS
Sigurd Bench from Ikea,
30 m cowhide round belts
diameter 4 mm, leather off-cuts
of natural cowhide 3 mm thick,
small steel nails, craft glue

TOOLS
Hammer, craft knife

Leather Pouf

You can never have enough seating at home!
This elegant pouf does the job beautifully.

LEVEL 02–03   TIME 03–04 H   COST 06

Step 01 / Draw an irregular pentagon on craft paper – this will
be the top and bottom of the pouf. Mark a seam allowance (at
least 1 cm) all around. Construct the sides by extending each
side of the pentagon to a rectangle. Make sure every rectangle
is of the same height. Don't forget the seam allowances.

Step 02 / Trace the pattern for all the side pieces onto the
leather and cut out with scissors or a craft knife. Trace one
pentagon onto leather and the other onto fabric.

Step 03 / Sew a zip along one side of the fabric pentagon.

Step 04 / Glue all parts together at the seams to assemble the
pouf. The glue will bond the material very securely, but it won't
hurt to sew the seams for reinforcement if you intend to use the
pouf a lot.

Tip / Fill the pouf with a mixture of polystyrene beads and foam
flakes.

MATERIALS
Large leather piece ca. 1.7 m²,
sturdy fabric, ca. 80 × 80 cm,
1 roll craft paper, pencil,
strong glue, matching sewing
yarn, concealed zip,
filling material

TOOLS
Craft knife or scissors,
straight edge, sewing machine

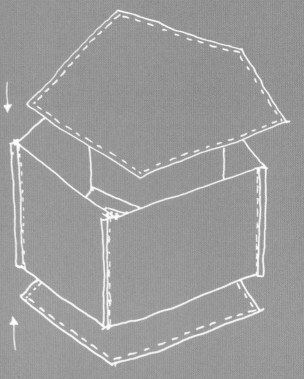

04

Paper
Cardboard

Thorny
Branch

Paper thorns and leaves turn a solitary branch into
a work of art.

LEVEL 01   TIME 01 H   COST 02-03

Step 01 / Cut 3-6 cm circles from paper and pull them sharply
over the cutting edge of a pair of scissors. This will make them
roll up.

Step 02 / Shape the paper rolls into pointed cones and fix into
position with glue.

Step 03 / Cut the paper thorns to the desired length. Snip into
the bottom a few times every 1-2 cm, bend the rim slightly
outwards and glue the thorns to the branch.

Step 04 / For the leaves, cut strips of paper, fold them
lengthwise and draw a leaf outline on one side. The fold will
serve as the spine. Cut out the leaves, leaving a small flap on
one side of the base. Attach the leaves to the branch with the
flaps.

Step 05 / When all the thorns and leaves are glued to the
branch and have dried, apply a coat of white thinned-down
emulsion paint to the whole creation.

Tip / For a very special advent bouquet, decorate the branch
with glass baubles.

MATERIALS
Dry branch, paper, pencil, all-
purpose glue, white emulsion
paint

TOOLS
Scissors, paintbrush

Honeycombs

Does your room need a splash of colour? Try this honeycomb design made out of wallpaper scraps.

LEVEL 01   TIME 02 H   COST 02

Step 01 / Draw a regular hexagon in the desired size on cardboard and cut it out with a craft knife.

Step 02 / Use this template to trace the shape on the back of wallpaper in different designs and colours. Use a pair of scissors or a craft knife and a cutting board to cut out the shapes.

Step 03 / Prepare wallpaper paste according to the manufacturer's instructions. Spread the glue on the back of the hexagons.

Step 04 / Glue the hexagons to the wall. They should be evenly spaced.

Tip / Add extra interest by applying the shapes to the wall in an asymmetric arrangement.

MATERIALS
Wallpaper scraps, wallpaper paste, pencil, cardboard

TOOLS
Scissors, craft knife, cutting board, set square

Cardboard Console

A piece of furniture or a modern art sculpture? This console is lightweight but sturdy, and the construction principle is endlessly variable.

LEVEL 01   TIME 02 H   COST 03

Step 01 / Cut out the components with a circular table saw or ask your carpenter to do it for you.

Step 02 / Carefully smooth the edges of the cardboard with middle-grain abrasive paper.

Step 03 / Assemble the console with hot glue.

Tip / Make the surfaces more resistant by sealing them with a thin coat of transparent acrylic varnish.

(Template on page 139.)

MATERIALS
2 sheets of honeycomb cardboard, 79 × 117.5 × 2 cm, hot glue, clear acrylic varnish

TOOLS
Circular table saw, hot glue gun middle-grain abrasive paper, varnish roller

Collages

Don't throw away used tickets, receipts or photos –
collect them to make them into works of art!

LEVEL 01   TIME 01 H   COST 02-03

MATERIALS

Different-sized frames in a
similar colour, different types
of paper, figurines, souvenirs,
luggage tags and whatever else
takes your fancy, pins, coloured
tape, paper glue

TOOLS

Scissors, craft knife

Step 01 / Arrange your collection of
paper scraps and miscellaneous objects
into still lifes in various box frames with
the help of pins, glue and coloured tape.

Step 02 / Arrange the frames on a shelf,
sideboard or occasional table.

Tip / For a harmonious effect, stick to
three colours only, for example black and
white combined with one accent colour.

Set of Vases

These vases made from cardboard may not be waterproof, but they are great for effect!

LEVEL 01   TIME 02 H   COST 01

Step 01 / Trace the template on page 138 in the desired size onto corrugated cardboard and cut out the shape with a craft knife on a cutting board.

Step 02 / Score the cardboard carefully with a craft knife along the fold line to allow the shaping of the vase. Make sure you cut into the top layer and the corrugated layer only.

Step 03 / Fold the vase into shape and secure on the inside with tape in the same colour as the cardboard.

Step 04 / Place the cardboard vases over glasses or vases of the appropriate size.

Tip / These vases look fantastic as a set of different sizes. If you like, you can paint and decorate them further.

MATERIALS
Corrugated cardboard, paper tape, pencil, glasses/vases in different sizes

TOOLS
Craft knife, straight edge, cutting board

Newspaper Tabletop

Homage to Piero Fornasetti: an elegant black-and-white table with animal shapes and crisp lettering.

LEVEL 01   TIME 03 H   COST 02

Step 01 / Collect international newspapers. Cut them into strips of different sizes, taking care to select the most beautiful lettering.

Step 02 / Prepare wallpaper paste to the manufacturer's instructions. Spread the paste on both sides of the strips and glue them to the tabletop. Allow to dry.

Step 03 / Copy animal motifs onto white paper and carefully cut them out with a sharp pair of scissors. Stick them to the dry surface with spray glue.

Step 04 / Seal the tabletop with several layers of high-gloss acrylic varnish. Leave to dry thoroughly between coats.

Tip / If you use repositionable spray adhesive, you can experiment until you are happy with the arrangement before committing yourself.

MATERIALS

Second-hand table , international newspapers, black-and-white animal images, wallpaper paste, spray adhesive, high-gloss water-based acrylic varnish, white paper

TOOLS

Scissors, paintbrushes

05
Fabric

Fabric Origami

Who would have thought that you can make origami shapes out of fabric scraps? With a simple trick, it is quite easy.

LEVEL 04　TIME 03 H　COST 01

Step 01 / Brush the fabric scraps with a 1:1 mixture of wood glue and water. This gives the fabric a paper-like texture and prevents it from fraying. Leave to dry thoroughly.

Step 02 / Cut the dried fabric into squares. Iron them flat on a cotton setting.

Step 03 / You can find very good video instructions for origami on the Internet – just choose a pattern and get going.

Tip / Give the finished shapes another coat of the glue-and-water mixture to make them even more stable.

MATERIALS
Fabric scraps, wood glue, water

TOOLS
Broad paintbrush, scissors, iron

Fabric Screen

A screen can hide a thousand things from view –
and look fantastic at the same time!

LEVEL 03   TIME 06 H   COST 05

Step 01 / Paint the plywood boards with emulsion paint on both sides and leave to dry.

Step 02 / Use spray adhesive to cover the boards with fabric scraps on both sides. Let the pieces overlap slightly. Leave to dry thoroughly.

Step 03 / Use different types of decorative nails to fasten the fabric to the board along the edges until you are satisfied with the overall effect.

Step 04 / Brush a coat of emulsion paint over the entire arrangement and leave to dry again.

Step 05 / Fasten the boards to each other with screen hinges.

Tip / Alternate strongly textured and smooth fabrics for a stunning relief effect.

MATERIALS
Fabric scraps/different textures, woodcore plywood 24 mm thickness, spray adhesive, emulsion paint, different types of nails, screen hinges and screws

TOOLS
Cordless screwdriver, paintbrushes, hammer

MATERIALS
Old upholstered chair,
fabric scraps, acrylic paint,
pattern paper, sewing thread,
brass upholstery nails, pencil

TOOLS
Fabric scissors, craft scissors,
seam ripper or craft knife,
sewing machine, iron, staple
gun, paintbrush

Patchwork Chair

Spare fabric scraps give an old and tired-looking chair a colourful makeover.

LEVEL 06   TIME 08 H   COST 04

Step 01 / Remove the old chair cover. Carefully unpick the seams with a seam ripper or a craft knife.

Step 02 / Iron the pieces flat and lay them out on pattern paper. Trace the outlines and cut out.

Step 03 / Cut the fabric scraps into rectangles. With a sewing machine, sew them first into strips, then into a large piece.

Step 04 / Place the pattern for the seat and back onto the patchwork fabric and cut out with a seam allowance.

Step 05 / Apply two coats of glossy acrylic paint to the legs.

Step 06 / Sew the fabric for the seat and the bottom of the seat together and pull them over the chair. Pull the fabric taut and staple to the inside bottom of the chair. Staple the fabric for the backrest to the back of the chair.

Step 07 / The last piece covers the entire chair back. Fasten it to the chair with upholstery nails along the visible seams.
Tip / You can give differently shaped furniture a unified look by using the same kind of fabric covers.

Patchwork
Carpet

One carpet, endless possibilities: You can cut and reassemble it whichever way you fancy!

LEVEL 03   TIME 07 H   COST 04

Step 01 / Fold the carpet over twice and mark the fold line on the back with a felt-tip pen. Iron strips of fusible webbing to the back of the carpet along the fold lines. Fold the carpet widthwise three more times to get twelve sections and repeat the process.

Step 02 / Cut the carpet into sections along the fold lines. The bonding fabric prevents the carpet from fraying.

Step 03 / In a large tub, prepare the fabric dye according to the manufacturer's instructions.

Step 04 / Put three pieces of carpet into the dye until the desired colour intensity has been reached. Remove, letting the water run off. Refill the tub to the old level and put in the next batch. Repeat the process until all pieces have been dyed. The dye bath gradually loses its colour pigment so that each batch is lighter in colour than the previous one. Leave to dry thoroughly.

Step 05 / Hem each of the carpet segments with blanket stitch. We have used neon pink wool yarn.

Step 06 / Sew the finished segments together on the reverse side.

Tip / You can add more dye and salt for each new batch if you would like the colour variations to be less pronounced.

MATERIALS
Off-white woven cotton carpet, 140 × 200 cm, neon pink wool yarn, fusible webbing ca. 8 m long and 8 cm wide, 1 – 2 boxes of fabric dye, water

TOOLS
Thick needle, felt-tip pen, scissors, iron, large tub

Pendant Lamp

Remember all those craft projects with balloons and tissue paper we did in school? The making of this lamp is the same principle.

LEVEL 04   TIME 06 H   COST 03

Step 01 / Prepare a 1:1 mixture of water and wood glue. Cut tissue paper and fabric into irregular triangles. Paste the paper triangles to the balloon until it is well covered. Make sure the paper lies flat and that no air bubbles are trapped underneath. Leave to dry thoroughly.

Step 02 / Brush the glue mixture onto the fabric triangles until they are completely soaked. Place them onto the balloon at irregular intervals. They should overlap but form regular smallish gaps. Leave to dry for at least 48 hours, then apply another coat of the glue mixture. Repeat this process once or twice more until the surface is stable.

Step 03 / Carefully let the air out of the balloon. With a sharp pair of scissors or a craft knife, cut out the tissue paper, showing the gaps in between the fabric triangles.

Step 04 / Assemble the lamp: cut a hole in a small plastic plate and attach a fine steel cable to the plate for suspension. Slip the plate onto a light socket and fasten with the screw top (see drawing). The electric cable can be loosely draped around the suspension cable.

Tip / If you are uncomfortable with electric installations, do ask an electrician to assemble your lamp.

MATERIALS
Balloon (round), fabric,
tissue paper, wood glue,
water, steel cable diameter 2 mm,
light socket, electric cable,
small plastic plate

TOOLS
Craft knife or scissors,
small bucket, paintbrush

Colour-graded Curtains

These curtains are as beautiful as a watercolour painting! They are easy to make but you do need a little bit of space for this project . . .

LEVEL 02   TIME 03 H   COST 02-03

Step 01 / Soak the curtains in water until well drenched, then hang them upside down from a washing line over a large tub. Ideally, they should not touch the ground. If this is not possible, try not to let more than 50 cm trail on the floor. Cover the floor with plastic to prevent the curtains from getting dirty.

Step 02 / Dissolve half of the dye in water and liberally paint onto the curtains. Stop about halfway down. The dye will then naturally bleed down into the bottom half.

Step 03 / When the dye has stopped moving, drench the curtains in water again. Wait until the water has settled, then paint the top third of the curtains with the undiluted dye.

Step 04 / For a crumpled look (as shown), scrunch the dry curtains into a ball before hanging.

Tip / For a special effect, apply eyelets along the top seam and suspend the curtains from long pieces of coloured string at a distance of 50 cm from the curtain rails.

MATERIALS
White cotton curtains, water,
750 ml ultramarine blue dye

TOOLS
Flat paintbrush ca. 100 mm,
clothes pegs, washing line,
plastic sheet, large tub

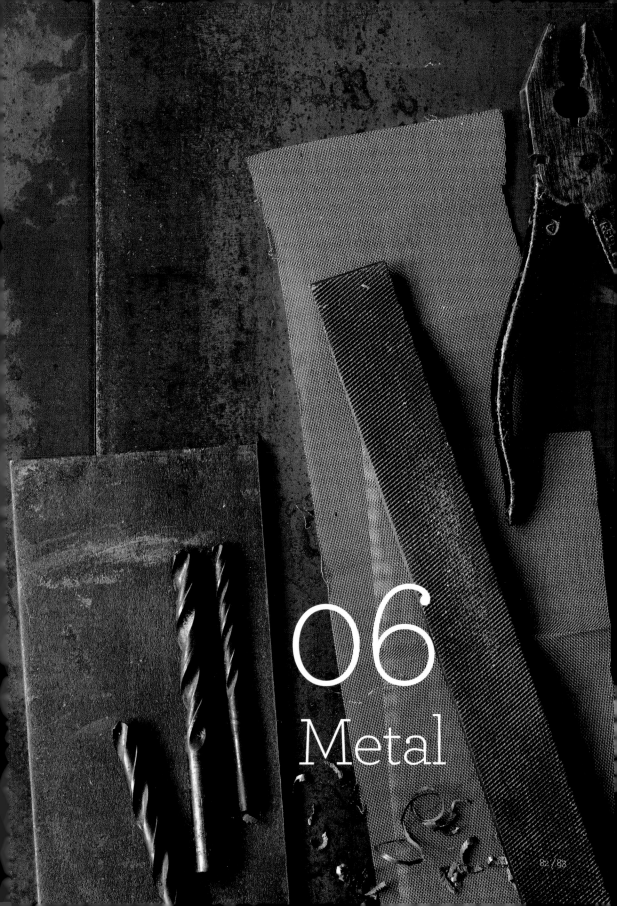

06
Metal

Trompe l'oeil Characters

It is hard to believe that these decorative 'metal' letters are actually made from painted cardboard!

LEVEL 02-03   TIME 03 H   COST 03

Step 01 / Print out letter patterns and enlarge them to the desired size on a photocopier. Crosshatch the outlines on the reverse side to make them more visible. This will work best on a white work surface.

Step 02 / Transfer the outlines onto cardboard with the help of a straight edge and a ballpoint pen. Cut out with a craft knife. Cut strips for the sides to the desired width. Score parallel lines on the inside for the soft curves. Mitre-cut the edges with a craft knife. Carefully glue the sides onto each letter with all-purpose adhesive. Leave to dry.

Step 03 / Paint the letters all over with metallic paint. Leave to dry then liberally apply a coat of oxidising agent. Apply a few drops of verdigris patina where the paint puddles. Leave to dry thoroughly again.

Tip / You may need a bit of practice with the verdigris patina. Make a few trial runs on some scrap cardboard.

MATERIALS
Thick cardboard, metal paint, oxidising agent, verdigris patina, all-purpose adhesive

TOOLS
Craft knife or scissors, paint brush, straight edge, ballpoint pen, computer, printer, photocopier

Wire Mesh Paper Basket

You just need a plastic bucket and a few yards of wire to create this ultra-classy vintage-style wastepaper basket!

LEVEL 03   TIME 03 H   COST 02

Step 01 / Cut off the rim of the bucket with strong household scissors or a craft knife.

Step 02 / Drill holes all around the bin, 5 cm in from the rim. NB: It must be an even number of holes!

Step 03 / Cut the wire into equal lengths and pull through two holes at a time.

Step 04 / Alternating the pairs each round, twist two wires at a time twice around each other at the same distance from the rim. The resulting mesh will resemble chicken wire. To create a cone shape, make the mesh holes in each new round slightly bigger than the previous round.

Step 05 / When the mesh is high enough, shape the stronger wire into a ring. Attach it to the mesh by winding the loose ends around IT at regular intervals.

Tip / Try varying the spacing and size of the mesh loops to create different patterns.

MATERIALS
Plastic bucket,
binding wire 20 m,
rod wire diameter 5 mm

TOOLS
Craft knife or scissors,
electric drill and metal drill bit
diameter 2 mm

Steel Pinboard

Flat steel is practically indestructible and has a beautifully bluish-black surface. It really is far too beautiful not to use in the house!

LEVEL 01   TIME 01 H   COST 03

Step 01 / Have the flat steel cut to measure. Smooth the edges with a metal file. Drill a hole in the centre of each end 8 cm in from the edge with a metal drill bit. Place the steel on a piece of wood for drilling. Use oil as a lubricant and be sure to keep the drill perfectly straight to prevent jamming.

Step 02 / Cut two small wooden blocks and drill a hole (ø ca. 6 mm) in the centre of each and paint them black.

Step 03 / To protect the steel surface, dilute beeswax with a little turpentine to a thick paste and buff with the mixture until it is well coated. Use a soft, lint-free cloth.

Step 04 / If you wish to attach the steel strip to the wall at both ends, use the wooden blocks as spacers. For a leaning effect, attach the flat steel only at the top end and bevel the spacer to fit the angle.

Tip / If you prefer, you can also attach the steel strip horizontally, for example to the wall behind your desk. The drill holes should be spaced 60 cm apart.

MATERIALS
Flat steel 10 × 0.5 cm
(featured length: 230 cm)
2 wood blocks ca. 7 × 7 × 3 cm,
beeswax, turpentine,
black acrylic paint,
piece of wood, some oil

TOOLS
Metal file,
electric drill and metal drill bit
diameter 6 mm,
paintbrush, saw, cloth

MATERIALS
Aluminium, brass or copper
mesh (mesh size max. 0.2 mm),
pins with metal heads,
sewing thread, paper, staples

TOOLS
Household scissors, sewing
needle, waterproof felt-tip pen,
computer, printer, staple gun

Wire Mesh Figurines

Using fine metal mesh instead of the intended paper or cardboard makes these figurines look almost ethereal . You can find patterns on the Internet.

LEVEL 01   TIME 02 H   COST 02

Step 01 / Print out your chosen pattern on paper.

Step 02 / Place the wire mesh over the pattern and trace the outline with a felt-tip pen. Cut out the shapes with strong household scissors.

Step 03 / Shape the pieces according to the instructions. Assemble the sculpture using pins, staples or needle and thread.

Tip / In order to be reasonably stable, mesh sculptures should not be too large.

Clothes Rail

Practical and flexible: a hanging rail with a smart industrial look.

LEVEL 01   TIME 02 H   COST 04–05

Step 01 / Have the MDF board cut to measure in the DIY shop. Seal it with several coats of Black high-gloss acrylic paint. Leave to dry thoroughly.

Step 02 / Attach the casters to the MDF board with wood screws.

Step 03 / Assemble the rail with two 90° tube connectors. Attach it to the MDF board with the floor bracket.

Step 04 / Make sure to tighten all screws with the allen key.

Tip / Add more connectors for extra shelves and rails.

MATERIALS
Galvanised ¾ inch steel tubing
(cut to measure at the shop),
2 cast-iron tube connectors 90°,
2 cast-iron floor brackets,
1 MDF board 60 × 120 × 3 cm,
black acrylic paint, 4 casters,
wood screws

TOOLS
Allen key, cordless screwdriver,
paintbrush

Side Tables

Ultra-cool side tables made from simple tripod trestles – and they are even adjustable!

LEVEL 02   TIME 03 H   COST 02-03

Step 01 / Heat the paint on the tripod with the help of a blowtorch until bubbles form, then vigorously scrub with a steel brush. Repeat the process until all the paint has been removed. NB: Wear a mask and/or work outside to avoid breathing in noxious fumes.

Step 02 / Secure the tripod in a bench vice and bend the upper part straight. Drill two holes on each side of the metal bracket (see sketch below).

Step 03 / Paint the wooden disc with black high-gloss acrylic paint on both sides and leave to dry.

Step 04 / Screw the wooden disc to the metal bracket (see sketch below).

Tip / Instead of removing the old paint, spray the tripod with hammer finish enamel for an equally 'industrial' effect!

MATERIALS
Metal trestle tripod,
solid pinewood disc,
diameter 40 cm,
black acrylic paint,
wood screws, metal bracket

TOOLS
Blowtorch with gas cartridge,
steel brush, bench vice, cordless
screwdriver, electric drill and
drill bit diameter 6 mm,
paintbrush

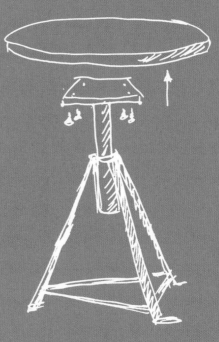

07
Stone

Quartzite Tray

Natural stone crazy paving is very robust – ideal as trays for serving hot drinks and food. You can find it in different shapes, sizes and materials.

LEVEL 01   TIME 01 H   COST 02

Step 01 / Attach self-adhesive felt pads strategically to the underside of the stone slab.

Step 02 / Mix two-component natural stone adhesive according to the manufacturer's instructions. Glue the wardrobe handles to the stone slab as shown. Leave to harden for at least 24 hours to allow the adhesive to bond with the stone properly.

Tip / If you want the handles to be rock solid, ask the stonemason to drill holes into the slab according to your instructions. Attach the handles with plugs and screws.

MATERIALS
Quartzite slab, vintage wardrobe handles, two-component stone adhesive, self-adhesive felt pads

Concrete Lamp Base

This structure looks highly complicated, but, once you have got the hang of it, it is dead easy to make.

LEVEL 06   TIME 04 H   COST 04

Step 01 / Draw 25 equilateral triangles (6 x 6 x 6 cm) on the PVC sheet and cut out with a craft knife. Cut the same number of triangles, slightly smaller in circumference, from the cardboard. Since one of the triangles will serve as the top of the mould, you will need to drill a hole for the lamp base in the centre.

Step 02 / Arrange 18 triangles (with 2 mm distance from each other) to form a rhomboid and connect them along the seams with tape. Do this on both sides. On one side, attach a cardboard triangle to each PVC triangle with tape. They serve as a structural reinforcement.

Step 03 / Fold the rhomboid into a three-dimensional figure by folding the two adjacent tips on the long side over to the opposite single tip on the short side. Secure with Sellotape.

Step 04 / Place the hollow figure over the lamp base. Attach the bottom triangle securely with parcel tape.

Step 05 / Mix the cement according to the manufacturer's instructions. Add some pigment if desired. Pour the cement into the hollow form, taking care to keep the lamp base in the centre of the mould. Shake the mould intermittently to remove the air bubbles. When the mould is full, thread the last triangle over the lamp base and lightly press onto the cement.

Step 06 / Leave to set for 24 hours. Remove the PVC mould.

Step 07 / Remove the bottom triangle and attach felt pads.

Tip / You can vary the colour and texture of the concrete by adding pigment or different types of gravel.

(Template on page 136.)

MATERIALS

1 PVC sheet, rigid, transparent,
1.5 mm thickness, cardboard
2 mm thickness, concrete, black
tinting paint, lamp base with
socket (45 cm high), Sellotape,
parcel tape, felt pads

TOOLS

Craft knife, set square, bucket,
mixing staff, pencil, electric drill
and drill bit

Concrete Shelf

You can revamp many different objects with cement-based decorative finishing render. The plastic content makes this material flexible and chip-free.

LEVEL 05   TIME 05 H   COST 05–06

Step 01 / Cut the plastic sheet to cover all parts of the structure, including the edges.

Step 02 / Mix a part of the render according to the manufacturer's instructions to the texture of firm cake dough. Mix with emulsion paint to the desired colouring. Work quickly and in batches, as the render will set very quickly. Start with small batches to get a feel for the drying time.

Step 03 / Cover the screw holes with Sellotape. Spread the render with a spatula evenly over all parts of the shelf, but leave out the parts with the screw holes.

Step 04 / Press the plastic sheets lightly and evenly onto the corresponding surfaces and leave to dry overnight. Then remove the plastic sheets and carefully trim off the surplus render with a craft knife.

Step 05 / Assemble the shelf.

Tip / For an easy-to-clean surface, seal the shelf with beeswax.

MATERIALS

Ikea Lack shelf, 5 kg cement-based decorative finishing render, black emulsion paint, water, plastic sheeting ca. 0.5 mm x 6 m x 40 cm, Sellotape

TOOLS

Mixing bowl, spatula, craft knife or scissors, straight edge

Candle Cups

These candle holders are really easy and fun to make – why stop at just one?

LEVEL 01   TIME 01 H   COST 01

Step 01 / Mix plaster and water in the rubber bowl to a smooth paste. Add a tiny amount of colour tint.

Step 02 / Fill a plastic drinking cup to about two thirds with the plaster and press a second cup down inside it until the plaster paste starts to overflow. Weight down the inside cup to keep it in position.

Step 03 / After a few minutes, the plaster will have set enough to remove the cups. The easiest way is to cut the cups open with a craft knife, then carefully peel them off the plaster.

Step 04 / Leave the plaster cup to dry overnight. The surface should feel completely dry.

Step 05 / Coat the inside of the cup evenly with the gilding size and leave for a little while until the surface feels dry. With a small paintbrush, place pieces of the aluminium leaf inside the cup and tamp down. When the whole surface is covered, buff it with a piece of cotton wool to remove the excess metal leaf.

Tip / You can also use copper or brass leaf for a completely different visual effect.

MATERIALS
Modelling plaster, tinting paint, plastic cups, aluminium leaf, gilding size, cotton wool, water

TOOLS
Paintbrush, spatula, rubber plaster mixing bowl, craft knife, weight/block of wood

Malachite Box

This cube-shaped side table is a gem of a trompe l'oeil piece. The expression means 'trick the eye', which is exactly what you are doing here.

LEVEL 03   TIME 03 H   COST 03

Step 01 / Mitre-cut the laminated particleboard to the desired measurements and glue the parts together along the seams to form a table. Secure with Sellotape until dry.

Step 02 / Remove the tape and smooth the edges gently with abrasive paper.

Step 03 / Cut two or three different-sized 'tools' from the multi-skin sheet, 3–6 cm in width and ca. 3 cm in length.

Step 04 / Paint one side of the cube with green emulsion paint and work over the wet paint with the 'tools' in uneven concentric circles to create a malachite effect. Brush off excess paint into a piece of cloth. Cover all five sides of the cube in this way and leave to dry.

Step 05 / Seal the surface with high-gloss varnish.

Tip / If you remove individual 'ribs' of the multi-skin sheet with a craft knife, the effect will be even more authentic.

MATERIALS

1 small piece of multi-skin sheet (3 mm thickness), green emulsion paint, water-based high-gloss varnish, laminated particle board, 4 pieces of 30 × 50 × 1.2 cm and 1 piece of 50 × 50 × 1.2 cm, wood glue, Sellotape

TOOLS

Paint brush, circular table saw, craft knife abrasive paper, cloth

Paper Weights

Put your favourite beach pebbles to good use to keep your desk organized.

LEVEL 01   TIME 01 H   COST 01

Step 01 / Select a font you like from your word-processing program and print it out in the desired size. Cut out the letters using sharp scissors.

Step 02 / Coat the backs of the letters with repositionable spray adhesive and place on the stones.

Step 03 / Wind string or lace a few times around each stone and secure with Sellotape on the back if necessary.

Step 04 / Carefully coat the stones with a thin layer of spray paint. Take care not to allow drops to pool underneath the string or lace.

Tip / The possibilities for experiments with different materials are endless. Do a few trial runs on cardboard until you are happy with the result.

MATERIALS
Large beach pebbles, lace scraps, string, paper, repositionable spray adhesive, Sellotape, spray paint

TOOLS
Compuer and printer, sharp scissors

Link to the Truth

08
Plastic

Window Screen

With a few strategically placed strips of coloured adhesive film, you can protect your room from unwanted outside attention – to a stunning effect!

LEVEL 01   TIME 02 H   COST 02

Step 01 / Cut the film into strips of different lengths, varying in width from 5 – 10 cm.

Step 02 / Spray window-cleaning liquid liberally and evenly over the entire window.

Step 03 / Remove the backing from the plastic film and position the first strip on the window. Press the liquid out from underneath with the help of a squeegee until all the air bubbles have escaped and the film adheres tightly to the window.

Step 04 / Repeat Step 03 until you are satisfied with the result. Let the different colours slightly overlap in places to create extra interest.

Tip / If you want the window to be completely opaque, use matte translucent film instead of transparent film.

MATERIAL

Transparent or translucent adhesive film in different colours, window-cleaning liquid

TOOLS

Craft knife, set square, squeegee

Wall Lights

Whether individually or en masse – these stylish wall lights always create an impressive effect.

LEVEL 01   TIME 02 H   COST 04

Step 01 / Determine the diameter of the light fitting and cut a corresponding hole in the centre of the plastic shapes. Make the fit is as tight as possible to allow the shapes to hold their position without extra help.

Step 02 / Push the shapes into the light fittings. Cover the inside of the light fittings with masking tape and spray the whole thing with copper or brass metallic spray. Leave to dry.

Step 03 / Spray a very fine mist of black over all surfaces. This creates a vintage look and makes the lights appear more three-dimensional.

Step 04 / Connect the cable to the light sockets or ask an electrician to do this.

Tip / The shapes should be large enough to allow the air to circulate, which prevents the plastic from overheating. When in doubt, consult an electrician.

MATERIALS

Plastic wall light fitting E27, braided electrical cable, pudding molds and cake racks, spray paint in black, copper and brass, 40-W E27 bowl reflector lightbulb, masking tape

TOOLS

Cordless screwdriver, craft knife

Painted Desk

Who says a picture has to hang on the wall? It can look just as stunning as a desk surface.

LEVEL 02   TIME 03 H   COST 06

Step 01 / Choose a painting and select a section to cover your desk. The section should be about 10 cm larger on all sides than the desktop. Have the motif printed onto self-adhesive film.

Step 02 / Place the particle board carefully on a work surface and liberally spray washing-up liquid over the entire surface.

Step 03 / For this step, you need an extra pair of hands. Remove the backing from the film and carefully position it on the desk.

Step 04 / Remove the liquid and excess air bubbles with a squeegee. Bubbles that are impossible to remove can be carefully flattened after perforating them with a needle.

Step 05 / After you have finished the entire surface, smooth the excess down over the edges. Don't forget to apply washing-up liquid first. Use a craft knife to tailor the corners.

Step 06 / Assemble the table brackets and paint them in your chosen colour.

Tip / You can seal the desk surface with a couple of protective coats of solvent-free clear varnish.

MATERIALS

Self-adhesive film with chosen design, 2 table brackets
1 sheet laminated particle board 200 × 60 cm, acrylic varnish, water, washing-up liquid, paint

TOOLS

Squeegee, craft knife, needle, varnish roller, paintbrush

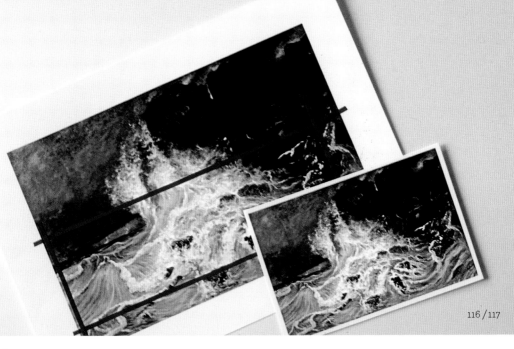

Rope Tray

This beautifully ethnic tray looks like the real thing, but instead of hemp we used poly hemp rope – it's easier to work with, and cheaper as well!

LEVEL 02   TIME 04 H   COST 03

Step 01 / Shape one end of the rope into a tight spiral, securing it every so often with a dab of hot glue.

Step 02 / Carry on coiling the rope around the centre. Thread the braided line through a large needle and sew two layers of rope together every few centimetres, pulling the work tight as you go. Don't place the stitches too close together.

Step 03 / Carry on stitching and gluing in this way. Prevent the rope coil from unravelling by gluing the rope layers together every 8 cm or so.

Step 04 / When the base is large enough (about 45 cm in diameter), start building up the border using the same stitching and gluing technique. To finish off, shape the end of the rope into a loop and glue to the rim of the tray. Secure the end with a few stitches and cut the braided line.

Tip / Seal the end of the poly hemp rope with a few dabs of hot glue to prevent it from fraying.

MATERIAL
15 m poly hemp rope diameter 16-mm, 35 m braided line diameter 3-mm, hot glue

TOOLS
1 large leather sewing needle, hot-glue gun

Neon Logo

Create a personal message as wall art with flexible
LED tubing. The possibilities are endless.

LEVEL 02   TIME 03 H   COST 02

Step 01 / Write the word 'you' on a piece of cardboard and trace it with the LED tube. Make adjustments if necessary. Enlarge the writing on the cardboard by 2 cm.

Step 02 / Trace the writing onto plywood and cut it out with a jigsaw.

Step 03 / Wind the neon-coloured fabric tape tightly around the LED tube until it is completely covered.

Step 04 / Stick the LED writing onto the plywood base with hot glue. Do this in small increments to allow the glue to dry properly.

Step 05 / Secure the LED-plywood sandwich by wrapping binding wire unevenly but tightly all around it (as shown).

Step 06 / Cut the acrylic board into triangles with a jigsaw. Smooth the edges with a file.

Step 07 / Cut the wire in 20 cm pieces. Heat one end over a lighter or a candle and quickly push it into an acrylic triangle. Wrap the wire around the sculpture when hardened.

Tip / Decorate the sculpture with beads or different acrylic shapes – the crazier the better!

MATERIALS
5 m LED tube,
coloured transparent acrylic
board 3 × 120 × 250 mm,
1 piece of plywood 70 × 120 cm,
neon-coloured fabric tape,
binding wire, cardboard
70 × 120 cm, hot glue

TOOLS
Jigsaw, wire cutter, hot-glue gun,
file, pencil, lighter or candle

Dotty Chest
of Drawers

Enhance a simple piece of flat-pack furniture
to create a stunning impact in a minimalist
environment.

Step 01 / Cut the adhesive film into 5 cm circles with a circle
cutter.

Step 02 / With the help of a pencil and a straight edge, draw
a grid onto the chest of drawers to facilitate the positioning of
the dots.

Step 03 / Remove the film's backing paper and stick the dots
to the chest of drawers one by one. Choose the colours
randomly.

Tip / For a random arrangement, you need more than three
different colours to avoid unwanted clustering.

MATERIALS
Adhesive film in assorted
colours, Malm chest of drawers
by Ikea

TOOLS
Circle cutter, pencil,
straight edge

Materials

Each material has very specific characteristics. While it can be interesting to force a particular material to do things it was not really meant to do, one does as a rule get the best results by following its nature. I have a large collection of sample boxes filled with the most diverse materials, textures and surfaces. I collect and file away everything that captures my interest. This does not only look very attractive, but it also helps me to develop new ideas.

Tools

Good tools are fundamental to the success of a project. A good tool does not have to be new – it is the quality that counts.
I own many old tools that I would never replace with new ones because these tools are not only beautiful, but extremely well made and effective. It really pays to spend a bit of money when buying a new tool – it will save you time, energy and ultimately a lot of money!

Credits

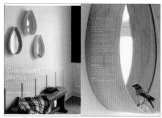

Cake Stand p. 14
Drill stand, drill: Bosch; aluminium tubing, threaded rod, washers, spray paint: DIY store; plates: flea market; china bird: Richard Hamburg; table and dishes: privately owned

Drop-shaped Mirrors p. 16
Jigsaw: Bosch; mirrors: glazier; balsawood strips 10 × 100 cm: timber trade; chipboard, power adhesive, tape: DIY store; china bird: Richard Hamburg; bench and blanket: privately owned

See-through Picture Frames p. 18
Glass: glazier; fabric tape, wire, all-purpose glue: Modulor; table, coffee pot: privately owned

Display Cases p. 20
Brass angular sections, transparent silicone, acrylic paint, wood glue, tape, tools: DIY store; bench: Ilmari Tapiovara via Artek; decoration: privately owned

Wall Plates p. 22
Transfer paper: Avery-Zweckform; plates: flea market; plate hooks, glue, tools: DIY store; plate designs: Vitra; dishes: privately owned

Chandelier p. 24
Braided cable, porcelain light socket: www.textilkabel.de; glass offcuts: glazier; silicone, tools: DIY store; armchair: privately owned

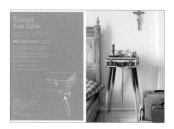

Suitcase Side Table p. 28
Cordless screwdriver: Bosch; table legs and brackets: timber trade; tool case, spray paint: DYI store; bed, decoration: privately owned

Inlaid Table p. 30
Table: flea market; veneer, wood glue and tools: Modulor; bird: Kay Bojesen via Rosendahl; sofa, lamp and cushions: privately owned

Table from Wood Offcuts p. 32
Jigsaw, cordless screwdriver: Bosch; furniture and decoration: privately owned

Banister Candlesticks p. 34
Drill: Bosch; banister rails: timber trade; acrylic paint, tools: DIY store; stool and chair: privately owned

Plank Bench p. 36
Jigsaw, cordless screwdriver, drill bits: Bosch; metal bracket, screws: DYI store; cushions and rug: Vossberg; decoration: privately owned

Tray with Marquetry Design p. 38
Marquetry bands, wood glue: timber trade; trays: craft store; varnish, tools: DYI store, decoration: privately owned

Herringbone Cushion p. 42
Leather: leather trade; wool felt, seam ripper, sewing thread, filling material: department store; armchair: privately owned

Polygonal Leather Boxes p. 44
Shoe leather, punch pliers, thread: leather trade; decoration: privately owned

Leather Flowers p. 46
Leather scraps: leather trade; vases: flea market

Leather Chair p. 48
Saddle leather: leather trade; chair: flea market; acrylic paint and tools: DIY store

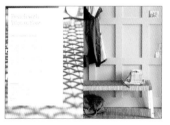

Bench with Woven Seat p. 50
Sigurd Bench: Ikea; cowhide round belts, leather scraps: leather trade; tools: DIY store

Leather Pouf p. 52
Leather: leather trade; fabric, sewing thread: department store; star: privately owned

Thorny Branch p. 56
Paper, emulsion paint, circle cutter, paint brush, scissors: Modulor; vases: privately owned

Honeycombs p. 58
Wallpaper, wallpaper glue and tools: DIY store; armchair: privately owned

Cardboard Console p. 60
Honeycomb cardboard: Modulor; hot-glue gun, circular table saw: Bosch; table lamp 'AJ': Louis Poulsen; picture: Olaf Hajek

Collages p. 62
Picture frames: Ikea; tools, paper: Modulor

Set of Vases p. 64
Corrugated cardboard: Modulor; wall-paper: 'Melisande'/Manuel Canovas

Newspaper Tabletop p. 66
Animal designs from the book *Das Naturalienkabinett* by Albert Seba, Taschen, Köln 2001; table: flea market; decoration: privately owned

Fabric Origami p. 70
Fabric scraps: department store; chair: Das 7. Zimmer

Fabric Screen p. 72
Cordless screwdriver: Bosch; wood-core plywood, tools: DIY store; fabric scraps: department store; hinges: hardware store; chair 'S 664': Thonet; lamp 'Cobra': Martinelli Luce

Patchwork Chair p. 74
Fabric: JAB Anstoetz; chair: flea market; upholstery nails, acrylic paint, tools: DIY store

Patchwork Carpet p. 76
Erslev rug: Ikea; neon-coloured yarn: department store; chair: Richard Hamburg; cushion: Vossberg

Pendant Lamp p. 78
Balloon: party supply store; wood glue, steel cable, electric cable, socket, tools: DIY store; decoration: privately owned

Colour-graded Curtains p. 80
Ready-made cotton curtains: Ikea; tinting dye, brush: Modulor; chair: privately owned

Trompe L'oeil Characters p. 84
Cardboard, oxidising agent, patina, power glue: Modulor; decoration: privately owned

Wire Mesh Paper Basket p. 86
Tools and materials: DIY store; stool and metal shelf: Das 7. Zimmer

Steel Pinboard p. 88
Flat steel: metal trade; tools: DIY store; desk 'Tanis': Ligne Roset; globe: Richard Hamburg; decoration: privately owned

Wire Mesh Figurines p. 90
Wire mesh: metal trade or DIY store; animal patterns: Canon Creative-Park, http://cp.c-ij.com/en/contents/1006/index.html

Clothes Rail p. 92
Galvanised steel tubing, cast-iron connectors and brackets: Modulor; cordless screwdriver: Bosch; MDF board, casters: DIY store; decoration: privately owned

Side Tables p. 94
Cordless screwdriver: Bosch; trestle tripods, blowtorch, wooden disc, acrylic paint, tools: DIY store; lamp 'AJ': Louis Poulsen; chair: Richard Hamburg

Quartzite Tray p. 98
Quartzite slab: stone mason; wardrobe handles: flea market; two-component stone glue, felt pads: Modulor; teapot, cups: Oschätzchen

Concrete Lamp Base p. 100
Hemma table lamp base: Ikea; PVC board, cardboard: Modulor; concrete, tools: DIY store; Deko: privately owned

Concrete Shelf p. 102
Lack shelf: Ikea; cement-based decorative finishing render: specialist shop; tools: DIY store; lamp 'Creneau': Ligne Roset; decoration: privately owned

Candle Cups p. 104
Plaster, emulsion paint, aluminium leaf, gilding size: Modulor; plastic cups: department store

Malachite Box p. 106
Circular table saw: Bosch; laminated particle board, emulsion paint, tools: DIY store; multi-skin sheet: Modulor; 'Panton-Chair': Vitra

Paper Weights p. 108
Large pebbles: beach or building trade; spray adhesive, tape, spray paint: Modulor

Window Screen p. 112
Translucent self-adhesive film, tools: Modulor; decoration: privately owned

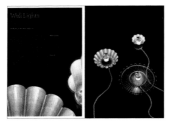

Wall Lights p. 114
Lamp sockets, tools: DIY store; pudding moulds, cake rack: department store; braided cable: www.textilkabel.de

Painted Desk p. 116
Self-adhesive film with printed-on design: 'Emblem-Monomer-Folie' by Kunstkopie.de / Image *Stürmisches Meer* bei Granville' by Paul Huet; desktop Vika Lerber and trestles Vika Amon: Ikea; decoration: privately owned

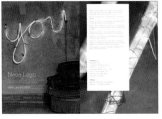

Rope Tray p. 118
Poly hemp rope, braided line: Hamburger
Taufabrik; hot-glue gun: Bosch;
decoration: privately owned

Neon Logo p. 120
LED tubing: Conrad Elektronik; hot-glue
gun, jigsaw: Bosch; acrylic sheet, fabric
tape: Modulor; plywood, tools: DIY store

Dotty Chest of Drawers p. 122
Circle cutter, self-adhesive film: Modulor;
Malm chest of drawers: Ikea; decoration:
privately owned

Addresses

Artek oy ab, Lönnrotinkatu 7, FI – 00120 Helsinki,
www.artek.fi

Avery Dennison Zweckform Office Products Europe,
Miesbacher Straße 5, 83626 Oberlaindern /
Valley, www.avery-zweckform.eu

Robert Bosch, Robert-Bosch-Platz 1,
70839 Gerlingen-Schillerhöhe,
www.bosch.de

Canon Creative-Park, http://cp.c-ij.com/de

Manuel Canovas, www.manuelcanovas.com

Das 7. Zimmer, Hegestraße 7 , 20249 Hamburg

Olaf Hajek, www.olafhajek.de

Richard Hamburg, Wexstraße 32A, 20355 Hamburg,
www.richardhamburg.com

Hamburger Taufabrik, Willy-Brandt-Straße 46,
20457 Hamburg,
www.hamburger-tauwerk-fabrik.de

Ikea, www.ikea.com

JAB Josef Anstoetz KG, Potsdamer Straße 160,
33719 Bielefeld, www.jab.de/en

Kunstkopie.de, Haferweg 46, 22769 Hamburg,
www.kunstkopie.de

Ligne Roset, www.ligne-roset.co.uk

Martinelli Luce Spa, Via Teresa Bandettini,
I-55100 Lucca, www.martinelliluce.it

Modulor, Prinzenstraße 85, 10696 Berlin,
www.modulor.de

Oschätzchen, Hohe Bleichen 26,
20354 Hamburg,
www.oschaetzchen.com

Louis Poulsen, www.louispoulsen.com

Rosendahl, Slotsmarken 1, DK-2970 Horsholm,
Denmark www.rosendahl.com

Taschen, Hohenzollernring 53, 50672 Cologne,
www.taschen.com

Textilkabel.de, Rothschildallee 11a, 60389 Frankfurt
am Main, www.textilkabel.de

Thonet, www.thonet.com

Vitra, www.vitra.com

Vossberg Versand, Paul-Sorge-Straße 63,
22459 Hamburg, www.vossberg.de

Thank You!

Magdalena Sordyl

Imke Apwisch
Angelika Bäuml
Otto Braun
Cuddl
Romann Fehrentz
Ute Heimrod
Birte Helms
Chrisch Hoffmeister
Roland Jank
Johannes Kemnitzer
Paul Köntopp
Gabriela Kost
Andreas Lichtenstein
Richard Lotzmann
Olaf Paul Paulsen
Thomas Petersen

Christine Schmid
Boerge Sierigk
Dirk Zilken

Aplanat Studios
Axis Mundi
Haller 6 Location
Play Rent Studios

Templates
Concrete Lamp Base

Chapter 07 Stone / p. 100

top

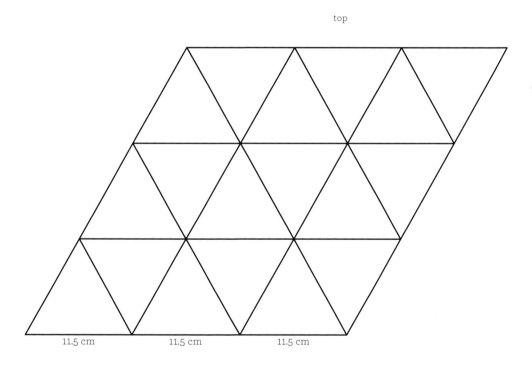

11.5 cm   11.5 cm   11.5 cm

bottom

Templates
Set of Vases

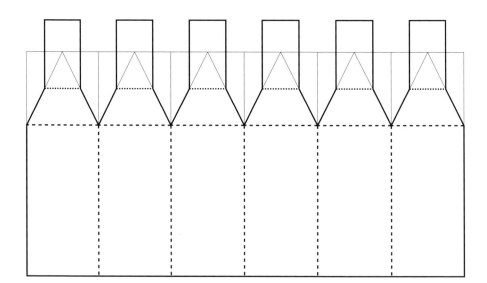

————————	Auxiliary line
– – – – – – –	Cutting line
················	Scoring outside
————————	Scoring inside

Templates
Cardboard Console

Chapter 04 Paper / Cardboard / p. 60

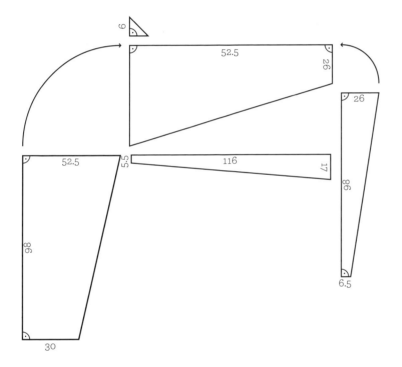

Measurements in cm

Peter Fehrentz

lives and works in Hamburg and Berlin. Since 1993, the qualified metal designer has been working for German and international magazines, as well as clients in the advertising and furniture design industry, as a freelance stylist, product and set designer, and photographer. For his first book, *Made by Yourself,* Peter Fehrentz has compiled 48 original projects that are easy and fun to replicate. His unique style is clearly visible, not only in the creations themselves, but also in the styling and photography of this book.

www.peterfehrentz.de

IMPRINT

First published in the UK in 2014 by
Jacqui Small LLP
An imprint of Aurum Press
74–77 White Lion Street
London N1 9PF
www.jacquismallpub.com

Copyright © 2012 Deutsche Verlags-Anstalt, München,
in der Verlagsgruppe Random House GmbH
Layout: Birte Helms, München
Photography: © Peter Fehrentz, www.peterfehrentz.de
Portrait of the author: © Boerge Sierigk

The author's moral rights have been asserted.

Publisher: Jacqui Small
Managing Editor: Lydia Halliday
Translator: Frauke Watson
Production: Maeve Healy

ISBN: 978 1 909342477

A catalogue record for this book is available from the
British Library.

2016 2015 2014
10 9 8 7 6 5 4 3 2 1

Printed in China